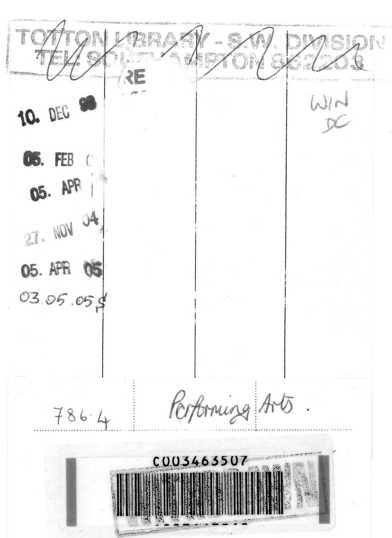

# Spirituals and Gospels.

Published by
Wise Publications
New York/London/Sydney.

# Spirituals and Gospels.

Book designed by Pearce Marchbank.
Cover photography by Brian Griffin.

Exclusive Distributors:
*Music Sales Limited*
8/9 Frith Street,
London W1V 5TZ, England.
*Music Sales Corporation*
257 Park Avenue South,
New York, NY10010, USA.
*Music Sales Pty Limited*
120 Rothschild Avenue,
Rosebery, NSW 2018,
Australia.

# Balm In Gilead.

*for ORGAN: Registration 2*

# By An' By.

*for ORGAN: Registration 2*

# Beulah Land.

*for ORGAN: Registration 4*

# Climbing Jacob's Ladder.

*for ORGAN: Registration 5*

# De Gospel Train
# (Git On Board, Little Children).

# Didn't My Lord Deliver Daniel?

*for ORGAN: Registration 4*

**Vigorously**

*D. %al fine*

# Deep River.

*for ORGAN: Registration 2*

# Down By The River Side.

*for ORGAN: Registration 3*

# Ev'ry Time I Feel De Spirit.

*for ORGAN: Registration 3*

# Give Me That Old Time Religion.

*for ORGAN: Registration 5*

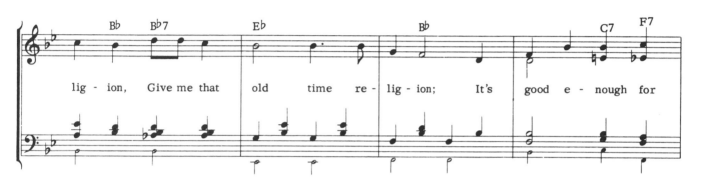

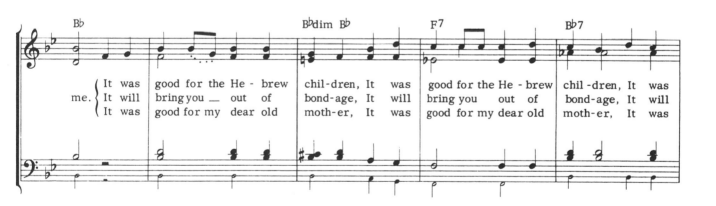

# Go Down, Moses.

*for ORGAN: Registration 3*

# Go Tell It On De Mountains.

*for ORGAN: Registration 2*

**Tempo rubato**

When I was a lear-ner, I sought both night and day, I
He made me a watch-man, Up-on the ci-ty wall, An'

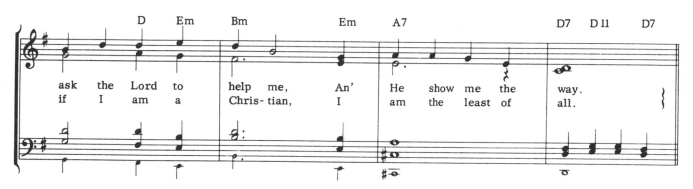

ask the Lord to help me, An' He show me the way.
if I am a Chris-tian, I am the least of all.

*CHORUS*

**Moderato**

Go tell it on de moun-tains, O-ver de hills an' ev-'ry-where.

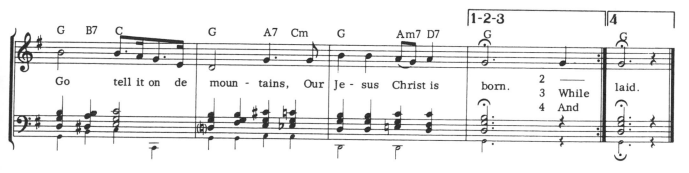

Go tell it on de moun-tains, Our Je-sus Christ is born.

**1-2-3**  |  **4**

2 ————
3 While laid.
4 And

3 While shepherds kept their watching,
O'er wand'ring flock by night;
Behold! from out the heavens,
There shone a holy light.

4 And lo! when they had seen it,
They all bowed down and prayed;
Then travel'd on together
To where the babe was laid.

# Great Day.

*for ORGAN: Registration 4*

# He Never Said A Mumbling Word.

*for ORGAN: Registration 3*

# He's Got The Whole World In His Hands.

*for ORGAN: Registration 5*

# I Got A Robe (Heav'n, Heav'n).

*for ORGAN: Registration 3*

# I'm A-Rollin'

*for ORGAN: Registration 4*

# I Stood On De Ribber Of Jordan.

*for ORGAN: Registration 3*

# In That Great Gettin'-Up Mornin'.

*for ORGAN: Registration 4*

# Just A Closer Walk With Thee.

*for ORGAN: Registration 2*

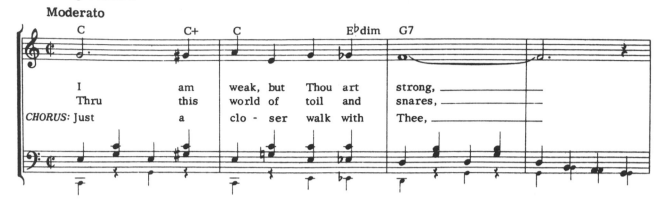

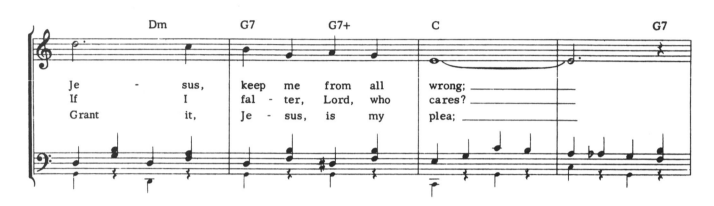

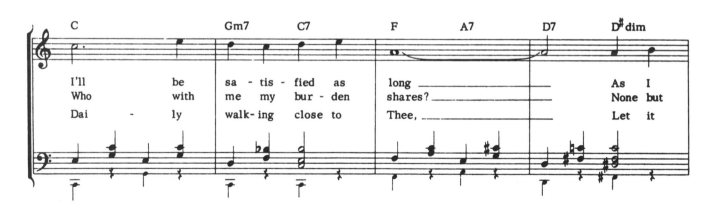

# Just As I Am.

*for ORGAN: Registration 2*

3  Just as I am, though tossed about
   With many a conflict, many a doubt.
   Fightings and fears within, without,
   O Lamb of God, I come! I come!

4  Just as I am, poor, wretched, blind;
   Sight, riches, healing of the mind,
   Yea, all I need in Thee to find,
   O Lamb of God, I come! I come!

*additional verse*

Just as I am, Thou wilt receive,
Wilt welcome, pardon, cleanse, relieve.
Because Thy promise I believe,
O Lamb of God, I come! I come!

# John Henry.

*for ORGAN: Registration 4*

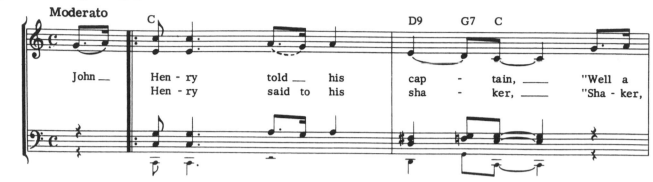

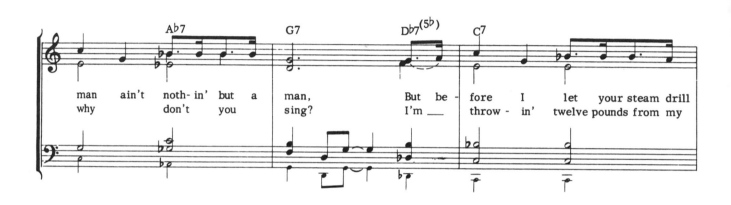

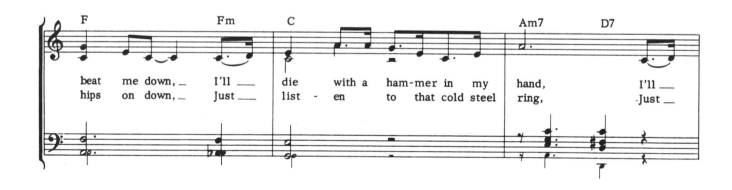

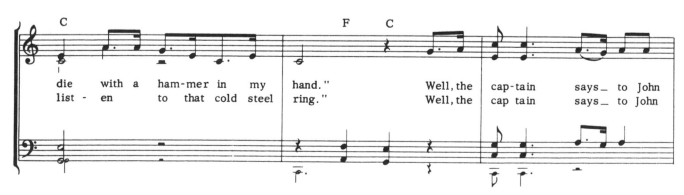

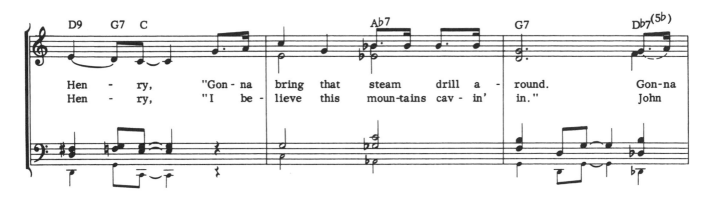

Hen - ry, "Gon - na bring that steam drill a - round. Gon-na
Hen - ry, "I be - lieve this moun-tains cav - in' in." John

take that steam drill out on the job, Gon-na whop that steel on
Hen - ry said to the cap - tain, "Tain't noth-in' but my ham-mer suck-in'

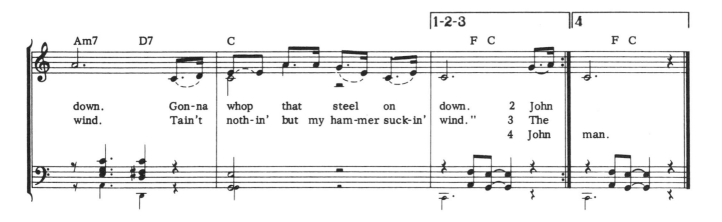

down. Gon-na whop that steel on down. 2 John
wind. Tain't noth-in' but my ham-mer suck-in' wind." 3 The
4 John man.

3 Henry had a little woman,
  And the dress she wore was red,
  She said, "I'm goin' down to the railroad track,
  I'm goin' where John Henry fell dead.
  I'm goin' where John Henry fell dead.
  They took John Henry to the buryin' ground,
  And they buried him in the sand.
  Every locomotive come roarin' round
  Says, "There lies a steel drivin' man,
  Says, "There lies a steel drivin' man.

# Joshua Fight De Battle Of Jericho.

*for ORGAN: Registration 4*
**Vigorously**

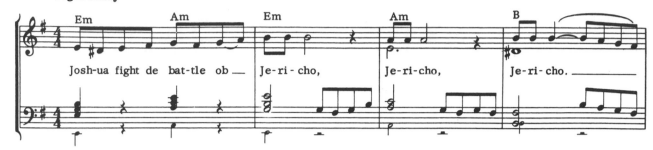

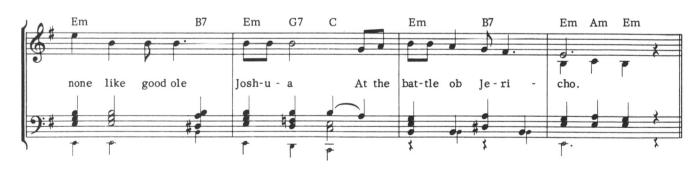

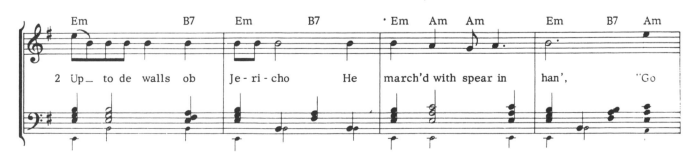

# Little David, Play On Your Harp.

*for ORGAN: Registration 3*
Brightly

# Michael Rows The Boat Ashore.

*for ORGAN: Registration 4*

# Motherless Child (Really Sees It Hard).

*for ORGAN: Registration 2*

# My Lord, What A Mornin'

*for ORGAN: Registration 4*
**Slowly**

# Nobody Knows De Trouble I See.

*for ORGAN: Registration 2*

# O Peter, Go Ring-A Dem Bells.

*for ORGAN: Registration 2*

# Oh, Didn't It Rain.

*for ORGAN: Registration 5*

# Oh, Sinner You'd Better Get Ready.

*for ORGAN: Registration 3*

# One More River To Cross.

*for ORGAN: Registration 2*

# Oh, Dem Golden Slippers.

*for ORGAN: Registration 4*

# Ride On, Moses.

*for ORGAN: Registration 3*

# Ring Them Bells.

*for ORGAN: Registration 4*

# Rock-A-My Soul.

*for ORGAN: Registration 2*

# Roll, Jordan, Roll.

*for ORGAN: Registration 3*

# Sometimes I Feel Like A Motherless Child

*for ORGAN: Registration 2*

# Standin' In The Need Of Pray'r.

*for ORGAN: Registration 4*

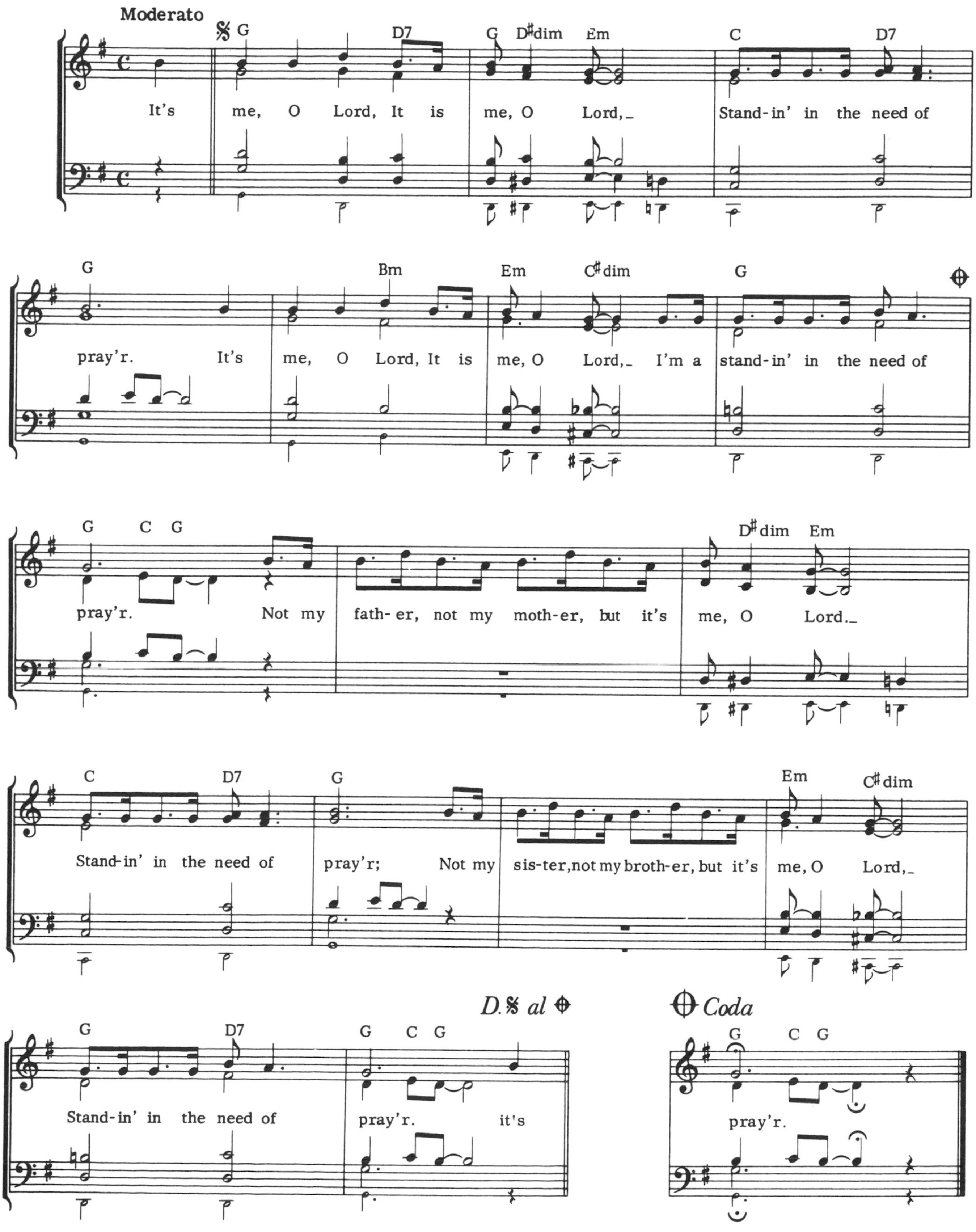

Moderato
G D7 G D♯dim Em C D7
It's me, O Lord, It is me, O Lord,_ Stand-in' in the need of
G Bm Em C♯dim G
pray'r. It's me, O Lord, It is me, O Lord,_ I'm a stand-in' in the need of
G C G D♯dim Em
pray'r. Not my fath-er, not my moth-er, but it's me, O Lord._
C D7 G Em C♯dim
Stand-in' in the need of pray'r; Not my sis-ter, not my broth-er, but it's me, O Lord,_
D.𝄋 al ⊕
G D7 G C G
Stand-in' in the need of pray'r. it's
⊕ Coda
G C G
pray'r.

# Steal Away To Jesus.

*for ORGAN: Registration 4*

# Swing Low, Sweet Chariot.

*for* ORGAN: *Registration 2*

# This World Is Not My Home.

*for ORGAN: Registration 2*
**Moderato**

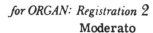

This world is not my home, I'm just a pass-ing thru, My
all ex-pect-ing me, And that's one thing I know,

treas-ures are laid up me, Some-where be-yond the blue; The
Sav-iour par-doned me, And now I on-ward go; I

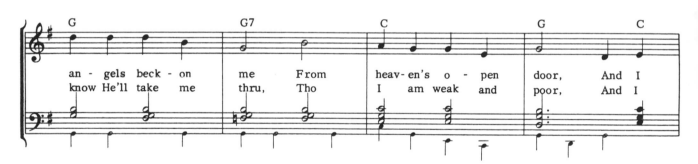

an-gels beck-on me From heav-en's o-pen door, And I
know He'll take me thru, Tho I am weak and poor, And I

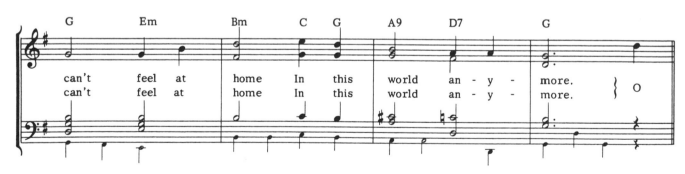

can't feel at home In this world an-y-more.
can't feel at home In this world an-y-more. } O

**CHORUS**

Lord, You know I have no friend like you, If

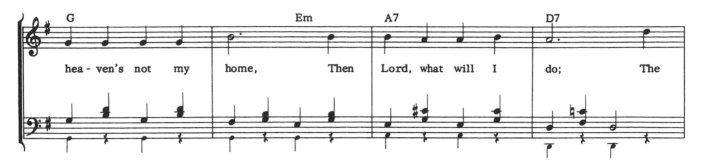

hea - ven's not my home, Then Lord, what will I do; The

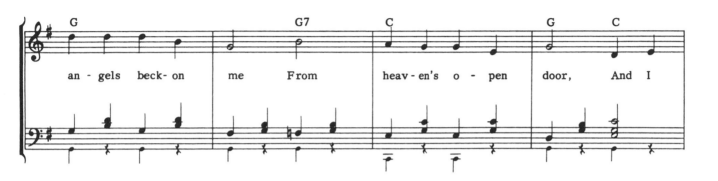

an - gels beck- on me From heav - en's o - pen door, And I

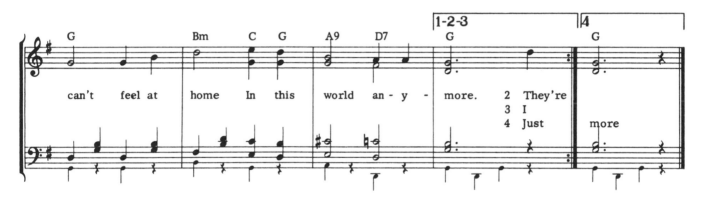

can't feel at home In this world an - y - more. 2 They're
3 I
4 Just more

3  I have a loving mother
   Up in Glory Land,
   I don't expect to stop until I shake her hand;
   She's waiting now for me
   In heaven's open door,
   And I can't feel at home
   In this world anymore.

4  Just up in Glory Land
   We'll live eternally,
   The Saints on ev'ry hand
   Are shouting victory,
   Their song of sweetest praise
   Drift back from heaven's shore,
   And I can't feel at home
   In this world anymore.

# Wade In De Water

*for ORGAN: Registration 3*

# Walk in Jerusalem Just Like John.

*for ORGAN: Registration 5*

# Weepin' Mary.

*for ORGAN: Registration 2*

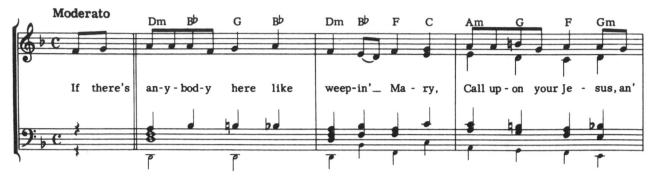

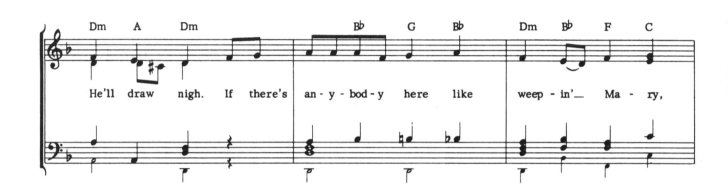

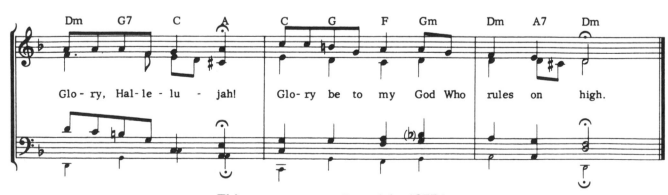

# Were You There?

*for ORGAN: Registration 2*

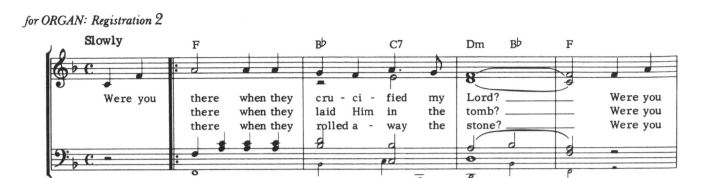

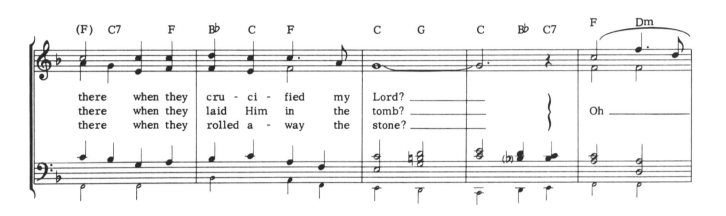

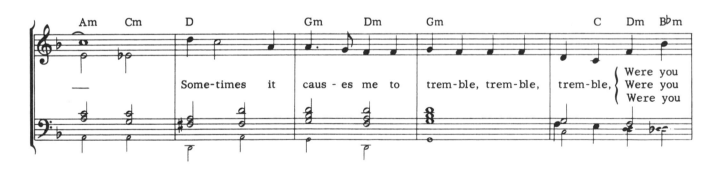

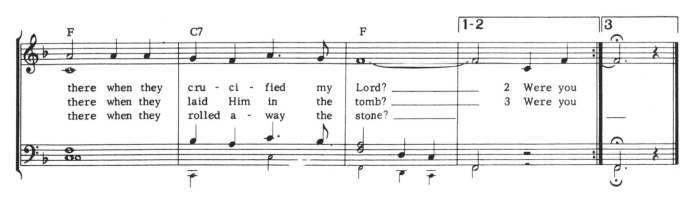

# (I'm Gonna Be There)
# When The Chariots Start To Roll.

*for ORGAN: Registration 3*

2   Now the Good Book states to the young and old,
    There are no cut rates when the chariot starts to roll

3   Gonna shine your crown when the church bells tolls,
    Then all gather round when the chariot starts to roll.

4   When the Lord on high begins to welcome the fold,
    He won't pass you by when the chariot starts to roll.

5   When that great day comes, what a sight to behold,
    I'll be right there when the chariot starts to roll.

# When The Saints Go Marching In.

*for ORGAN: Registration 5*

# When The Stars Begin To Fall.

*for ORGAN: Registration 4*

My Lord, what a morn-ing, My Lord, what a morn-ing, My—

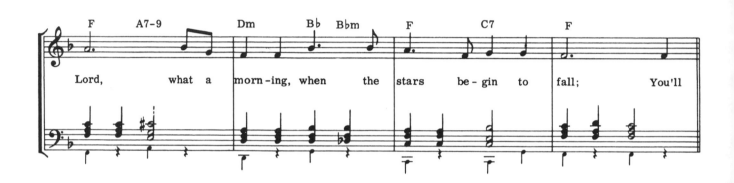

Lord, what a morn-ing, when the stars be-gin to fall; You'll

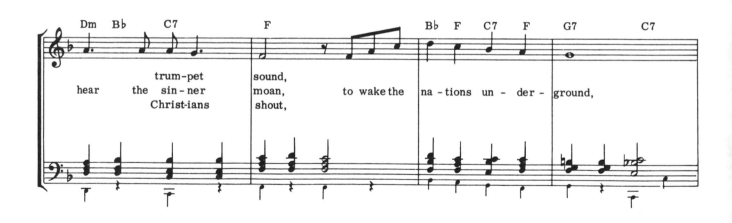

hear the sin-ner trum-pet sound, to wake the na-tions un-der-ground,
     the Christ-ians shout, moan,

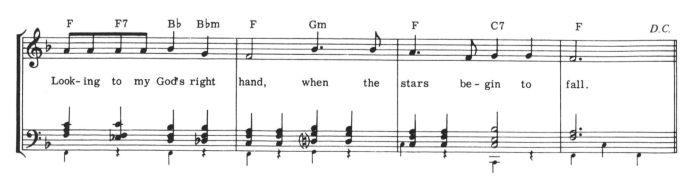

Look-ing to my God's right hand, when the stars be-gin to fall.

# 'zekiel Saw The Wheel.

*for ORGAN: Registration 3*

# Organ Registration Page.

| Registration No. | *Single - Manual Organs | *All Electronic Organs | | *All Drawbar Organs | |
|---|---|---|---|---|---|
| **1** | 8' 4' I II III | Upper:<br>Lower:<br>Pedal: | Flute 8'<br>Melodia 8'<br>8', Soft | Upper:<br>Lower:<br>Pedal: | 60 8808 000<br>(00) 5554 433 (1)<br>4-2 (Spinet 3) |
| **2** | 8' I II | Upper:<br><br>Lower:<br>Pedal: | Cello 16', Trumpet 8',<br>Flute 8', 4'<br>Reed 8', Viola 8' (String 8')<br>16', 8', Full | Upper:<br>Lower:<br>Pedal: | 40 8606 005<br>(00) 4543 222 (1)<br>4-2 (Spinet 3) |
| **3** | 8' 2' I III V | Upper:<br><br>Lower:<br>Pedal: | Flute 16', (Tibia 16'),<br>Clarinet 8', (Reed 8')<br>Diapason 8'<br>16', Soft | Upper:<br>Lower:<br>Pedal: | 60 8805 005<br>(00) 5544 321 (0)<br>4-2 (Spinet 3) |
| **4** | 8' 4' 2' I II III V | Upper:<br><br>Lower:<br>Pedal: | Flute 16', (Tibia 16'),<br>Flute 8'<br>Diapason 8', Melodia 8'<br>16', 8' Medium | Upper:<br>Lower:<br>Pedal: | 80 8080 800<br>(00) 6544 444 (2)<br>4-2 (Spinet 3) |
| **5** | 8' 4' II | Upper:<br><br>Lower:<br>Pedal: | Flute 16', (Tibia 16'),<br>Flute 8', Reed 8', Horn 8'<br>Melodia 8', Diapason 8'<br>16', 8' Full | Upper:<br>Lower:<br>Pedal: | 50 8806 006<br>(00) 5555 443 (3)<br>4-2 (Spinet 3) |
| **6** | 8' 4' 2' I II V | Upper:<br><br>Lower:<br>Pedal: | Flute 16', (Tibia 16'),<br>Flute 8', 4'<br>Diapason 8', Horn 8'<br>16', 8' Medium | Upper:<br>Lower:<br>Pedal: | 00 8080 600<br>(00) 4433 222 (0)<br>4-2 (Spinet 3) |
| **7** | 8' II IV V | Upper:<br>Lower:<br>Pedal: | Diapason 8'<br>Flute 8'<br>8' Medium | Upper:<br>Lower:<br>Pedal: | 60 8008 000<br>(00) 5544 000 (0)<br>4-2 (Spinet 3) |

* Vibrato and Reverberation left to personal preference

 Printed by Caligraving Limited Thetford Norfolk England 8/96 (25518)